Pra
With Mary

A Child's Book of the Rosary

This book belongs to

_____.

I am a member of the faith community of

_____ **parish**

in the city of _____.

Today's date is _____.

Draw or
glue a
picture of
yourself
in this box.

Pflaum Publishing Group
Dayton, OH
Milwaukee, WI

A note to parents and catechists

Faith is a wonderful gift to share with the children in your care. One of the best ways to share faith is to pray with them. You can pray together at mealtime, bedtime, class time, Mass time, or anytime. Perhaps you already do!

Our Catholic faith includes a rich tradition of prayer. This book will introduce your children to the Rosary. It is one prayer that includes many prayers. If possible, please provide a rosary for each of your children. Then this book—and the prayer itself—will come to life in their hands.

Text and activities by Jean Buell

First and foremost, Jean is a parent who wants her home to be a place of faith, hope, and love. In addition to parenting and writing, Jean facilitates worship and learning experiences for children and families in her home state of Minnesota. Other titles in this popular series for children include books on the Mass, Bible, saints, sacraments, and on making faithful choices. All are available from Pflaum Publishing Group.

Cover illustrations by Elizabeth Swisher
Interior design by Jean Buell and Kathryn Cole
Edited by Jean Larkin

Nihil obstat: Reverend Jim Schuerman, May 12, 2006
Imprimatur: †Most Reverend Timothy M. Dolan, Archbishop of Milwaukee, May 17, 2006

Where appropriate, this text reflects the language of the *Roman Missal, Third Edition.*

Eighth Printing June 2014

Pflaum Publishing Group
2621 Dryden Road, Suite 300
Dayton, OH 45439
800-543-4383
pflaum.com

ISBN 978-1-933178-38-7

Think About It!

Every day is filled with connections!
- Telephones connect us with family and friends.
- Photographs connect us with memories.
- The internet connects us to the world!

What other connections can you think of?

Every day, prayer connects us with God. And every day, things connect us with prayer. Anytime!
- Rainbows connect us with praise.
- Meals connect us with table grace.
- Candles connect us with quiet time.

A rosary connects us with prayer, too. Anytime! A rosary is a string of beads all connected together in a loop. These beads connect us to prayer in a BIG way. This prayer is the "rosary."

The rosary is full of connections! An important connection is this: The rosary connects us to Mary, the Mother of God. When we pray the rosary, we pray with Mary.

The rosary also connects us to our BIG Catholic family. In the past, our ancestors prayed with Mary. The rosary connects us to them. Today, Catholics everywhere pray with Mary. The rosary connects us to them, too. And, soon, you will be saying the rosary, too! This book will get you started. Soon you'll see all kinds of connections!

Use a pencil. Circle the word "connect" wherever you see it on this page. (It can be part of a bigger word.) Lightly shade in the circles. These are like beads. Now draw a line from circle to circle. This is like string. See how it connects the beads?

A Personal Connection

First of all, meet St. Mary! Mary was the mother of Jesus. She believed in him. She learned from him. She loved him as much as she could. And he loved her, too. Mary now lives forever with Jesus and all the saints.

Read John 19:26 27. Pretend you are standing next to Mary. What does Jesus say to you? What will you call Mary from now on?

A French Connection
(Lourdes, France; 1858)

When St. Bernadette was gathering firewood, Mary appeared to her. Mary was holding a rosary. So Bernadette took out her own rosary and prayed with Mary. People did not believe Bernadette's story. So Mary led her to a spring. Miracles happened when people touched the water. Then they believed!

Today there is a shrine at the spring. Many people visit to touch its healing water. Mary is known as "Our Lady of Lourdes."

A Mexi-connection
(Tepayac Hill, central Mexico; 1531)

When St. Juan Diego was walking to Mass, he saw someone dressed like an Aztec princess. She said she was Mary. She told Juan how much she loved the people. She asked him to have a church built there. The bishop did not believe Juan. So Mary left roses that Juan carried in his cloak to the bishop. When Juan opened his cloak, out fell the roses. When the bishop saw the roses and then saw Mary's image printed inside the cloak, he believed!

The church was built. Many people became Christians because of it. Mary is known as "Our Lady of Guadalupe."

A Global Connection

Mary has many names in many lands. Wherever we live, we can pray with Mary. Whoever we are, we can pray with Mary. She loves all people. She wants us to live as children of God. She is the "Queen of Peace."

Whenever you pray with Mary, think about this. First, write your name or initials in the center of this puzzle. Next, follow the arrow. Cross out every "K" and "V." Then write the message on the lines below.

_____

_____

_____

Now you're ready to learn about the rosary!

Pray With Mary

Basic Connections

What does a rosary look like? Gather all the rosaries you can. Ask your family members to bring theirs to the kitchen table. Ask your friends to bring theirs to religion class. Then tell one another about your rosaries. Some are connected to special memories.

Compare the rosaries. You might see many sizes, shapes, and colors. Choose one that interests you. Or design your own!

Make a ✔ by the words that describe your rosary.

What color is it?
___brown　　　　　　　___clear
___black　　　　　　　___glow-in-the-dark
___white　　　　　　　___other _____

Of what is it made?
___wood　　　　　　　___crystal
___plastic　　　　　　___sea shells
___ceramic　　　　　___other _____

What shapes are the beads?
___round　　　　　　___square
___oval　　　　　　　___other _____

How does it feel in your hand?
___smooth　　　　　　___heavy
___rough　　　　　　　___light

How big is it?

___small　　　___medium　　　___large

Prayer Counts!

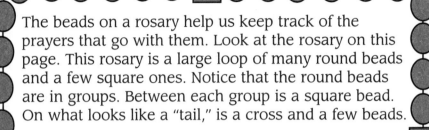

The beads on a rosary help us keep track of the prayers that go with them. Look at the rosary on this page. This rosary is a large loop of many round beads and a few square ones. Notice that the round beads are in groups. Between each group is a square bead. On what looks like a "tail," is a cross and a few beads.

How many beads are there in a rosary?
Follow these directions to find out.

Go figure!

a. How many groups are on the big loop? _____

b. How many beads are in each group? x _____

c. Multiply those two numbers and write the answer on this blue line. _____

d. Now, write the number of round beads on the tail. _____

e. Write the total number of square beads on the rosary, including those on the tail _____

f. Add the numbers on the three blue lines. This is the total number of beads on a rosary! _____

Do you know what each group of beads is called? Here's a hint. The word decade *means "a group of ten." Now do you know?*

7

Fill & Feel

A rosary connects our fingers to the beads. That is a good thing! When we pray, we give our "whole self" to God. The more we can pray with all our senses—touch, sight, hearing, taste, and smell—the better!

Place a flat facial tissue behind this page. Use a ball-point pen or a dull pencil. Carefully fill in each bead on this page. Fill in the cross, too. Press hard! Take a break if your hand gets tired.

When you are done, discard the tissue. Place this page between your thumb and forefinger. First feel the cross. Then feel the beads, one at a time.

When you pray the rosary, you will hold each bead between your thumb and forefinger.

- **First, you will hold the cross.**
- **Next, you will hold each bead on the tail.**
- **Then you will hold each bead around the loop.**

Careful Connections

Rosaries are called *sacramentals*. Candles, crosses, medals, palms, and other holy objects are also sacramentals. They remind us that God is near. Anytime! Be comfortable with your rosary. But be careful, too. It is sacred!

Oops! Someone was not careful with this rosary! Untangle it to find a message. Start at the arrow. Write the letters on the lines below.

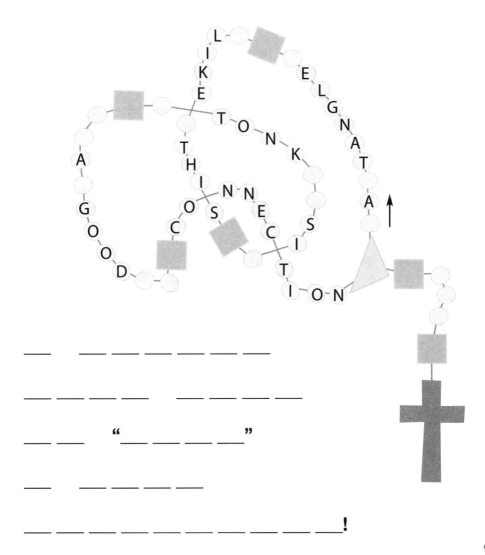

__   __ __ __ __ __ __

__ __ __ __   __ __ __ __

__ __   "__ __ __ __ __"

__   __ __ __ __

__ __ __ __ __ __ __ __ __ __ __!

Label & Learn

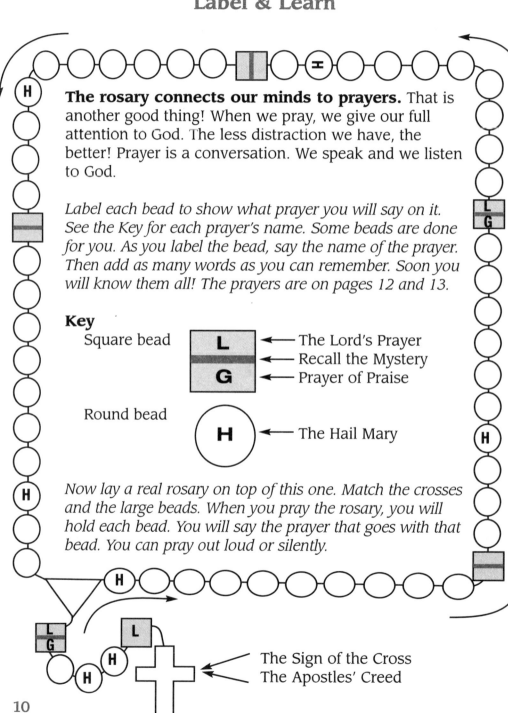

The rosary connects our minds to prayers. That is another good thing! When we pray, we give our full attention to God. The less distraction we have, the better! Prayer is a conversation. We speak and we listen to God.

Label each bead to show what prayer you will say on it. See the Key for each prayer's name. Some beads are done for you. As you label the bead, say the name of the prayer. Then add as many words as you can remember. Soon you will know them all! The prayers are on pages 12 and 13.

Key

Square bead

L ◄——— The Lord's Prayer
◄——— Recall the Mystery
G ◄——— Prayer of Praise

Round bead

H ◄——— The Hail Mary

Now lay a real rosary on top of this one. Match the crosses and the large beads. When you pray the rosary, you will hold each bead. You will say the prayer that goes with that bead. You can pray out loud or silently.

The Sign of the Cross
The Apostles' Creed

Creed Connections

We speak to God with the prayers of the rosary. By now, you might already know them! We praise God. We pray about our beliefs and our needs. We pray with everyone who follows Jesus. And we pray with Mary.

Using pages 12 and 13, find five important words in The Sign of the Cross that are also in The Apostles' Creed and the Glory Be to the Father. Write the letters for each of the five words in the squares below. Use one square for each letter. On the line below the word, write your own word or words that have the same meaning as the word in the squares.

1. ☐ ☐ ☐ ☐ ☐ ☐

_____

2. ☐ ☐ ☐

_____

3. ☐ ☐ ☐ ☐   4. ☐ ☐ ☐ ☐ ☐ ☐

_____

5. ☐ ☐ ☐ ☐

_____

The Sign of the Cross

In the name of the Father,

and of the Son,

and of the Holy

Spirit.

Amen.

The Apostles' Creed

I believe in God, the Father almighty,
   Creator of heaven and earth,
   and in Jesus Christ, his only Son, our Lord,
   who was conceived by the Holy Spirit,
   born of the Virgin Mary,
   suffered under Pontius Pilate,
   was crucified, died and was buried;
   he descended into hell;
   on the third day he rose again from the dead;
   he ascended into heaven,
   and is seated at the right hand of God the
      Father almighty;
   from there he will come to judge the living
      and the dead.

I believe in the Holy Spirit,
   the holy catholic Church,
   the communion of saints,
   the forgiveness of sins,
   the resurrection of the body,
   and life everlasting. Amen.

Prayer of Praise

Glory to the Father,
    and to the Son,
    and to the Holy Spirit.
As it was in the beginning,
    is now, and ever shall be. Amen.

The Lord's Prayer

Our Father, who art in heaven,
    hallowed be thy name;
    thy kingdom come,
    thy will be done
    on earth as it is in heaven.

Give us this day our daily bread,
    and forgive us our trespasses,
    as we forgive those
    who trespass against us;
    and lead us not into temptation,
    but deliver us from evil. Amen.

The Hail Mary

Hail Mary, full of grace!
The Lord is with you!
Blessed are you among women,
    and blessed is the fruit of
    your womb, Jesus.

Holy Mary, Mother of God,
    pray for us sinners,
    now and at the hour of
    our death. Amen.

Simple Connections

The rosary connects our minds to Scriptures. We know that a rosary connects our fingers to the beads. And it connects our minds to prayers. These are BIG connections! Now the connections get even BIGGER: The rosary connects our minds to Scriptures, too.

Scriptures are small stories from the Bible. Put together, these small stories tell one GREAT BIG story of God's love.

Do you think you could ever read the whole Bible? Maybe someday you will! For now, start with these simple connections. Find the passages and answer the questions.

1. *Read Luke 1:26-27.*
Who visits Mary?

_____

2. *Now read what the visitor says in Luke 1:28-31.*
Of which prayer from the rosary does this remind you?

_____

3. *Read Luke 11:1.*
What does the disciple ask Jesus?

_____

4. *Now read Jesus' answer in Luke 11:2-4.*
Of which prayer from the rosary does this remind you?

_____

A Clue for You!

Some Scripture stories tell about Mary and Jesus. Each decade (group) of the rosary is connected to one of these stories. They are BIG examples of God's love. They cannot always be explained or understood. They are described on the next few pages.

What are these small stories called? Hint: Hold this page side-ways. Close one eye. Line up the arrow with your open eye. Read the word!

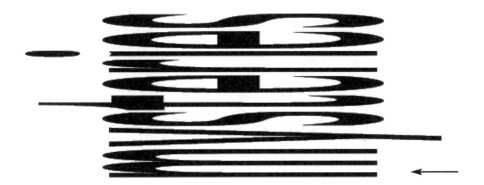

More Clues for You!

Every time you feel loved, you have another clue about God: God loves you that much and even more! These are your very own mysteries. They connect you to the GREAT BIG STORY of God's love. Look for more and more mysteries as you grow in faith.

Who loves you? _____

Pray With Mary

The **Joyful Mysteries** show us happy events in Mary's life. Color these mysteries with your favorite colors.

1. An angel tells Mary that she will have a baby.
Luke 1:26-38

2. Mary visits her cousin Elizabeth after the angel's visit.
Luke 1:39-45

3. Jesus is born in a stable in Bethlehem.
Luke 2:1-7

4. Jesus is presented to God at the Temple.
Luke 2:22-32

5. Mary and Joseph find Jesus teaching in the Temple.
Luke 2:41-52

Delightful Days

Jesus came into the world. He brought good news about God's love. That was the happiest event for Mary! It is the happiest event for us, too. Jesus is the "Light of the World."

You may not remember your baptism, but it was a very happy event. Your parents were given a special candle that day. Draw a picture of *what you think your baptism looked like.*
Whose light shines in this picture? _____

Draw your birthday. Add candles to the cake.
Whose light shines here? _____

The **Luminous Mysteries** show us important events from Jesus' mission. Color these mysteries with shining colors.

1. Jesus is baptized in the Jordan River.
Matthew 3:13-17

2. Jesus changes water into wine at a wedding in Cana.
John 2:1-11

3. Jesus proclaims the Good News. He wants us to believe.
Mark 1:14-15

4. Jesus' appearance changes on Mt. Tabor.
Luke 9:28-36

5. Jesus gives us the Eucharist at his Last Supper.
Luke 22:19-20

Guiding Light

Jesus still brings good news about God's love. He shows us how to live as children of God. He is our "Guiding Light." He helps us become guiding lights for one another.

Who shines the Light of Christ for you? Look at the picture clues on these candles. Imagine you are in those places. Who is there with you? Who shows you God's love? Write their names on the candles. They are your guiding lights! Can you think of others?

Pray With Mary

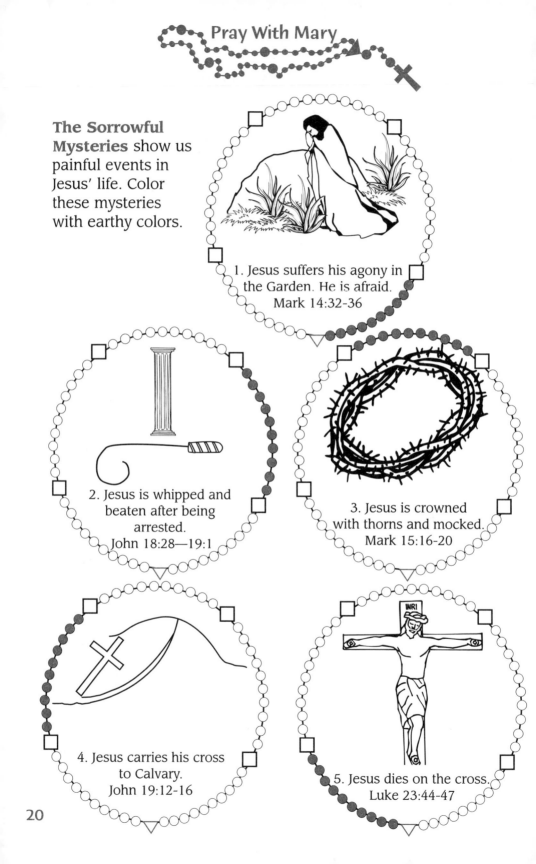

The Sorrowful Mysteries show us painful events in Jesus' life. Color these mysteries with earthy colors.

1. Jesus suffers his agony in the Garden. He is afraid.
Mark 14:32-36

2. Jesus is whipped and beaten after being arrested.
John 18:28—19:1

3. Jesus is crowned with thorns and mocked.
Mark 15:16-20

4. Jesus carries his cross to Calvary.
John 19:12-16

5. Jesus dies on the cross.
Luke 23:44-47

Night Light

Jesus suffered. He knows what all our struggles are like. Sometimes we think that things will never get better. But we can trust Jesus. He is our "Night Light" when things seem their darkest. We are never alone.

Feelings can be confusing. It helps to say what they are. Unscramble these feeling words. Then complete the sentences.

1. I feel **onelyl** _____ when _____.

2. I feel **urht** _____ when _____.

3. I feel **gryan** _____ when _____.

4. I feel **das** _____ when _____.

5. I feel **fadrai** _____ when _____.

Connect the dots. Do you have one of these at home? If you can, hang a cross on the wall above it. Remember, Jesus is always with you!

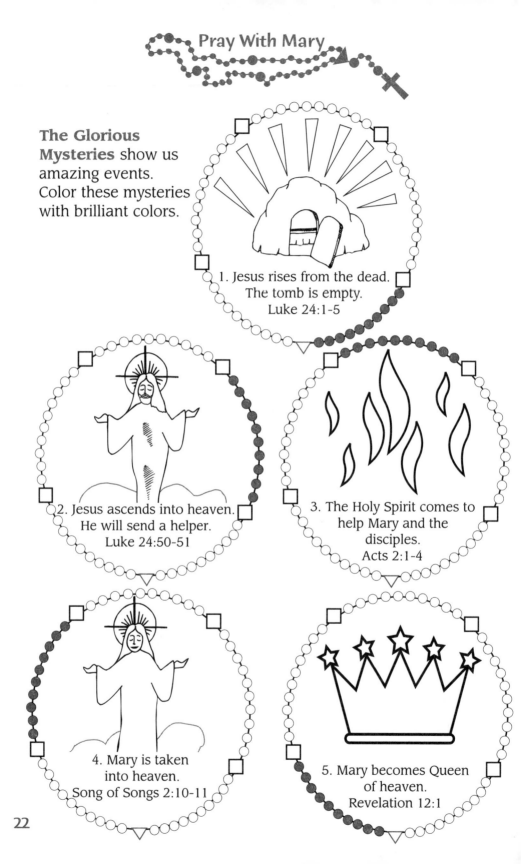

Pray With Mary

The Glorious Mysteries show us amazing events. Color these mysteries with brilliant colors.

1. Jesus rises from the dead. The tomb is empty. Luke 24:1-5

2. Jesus ascends into heaven. He will send a helper. Luke 24:50-51

3. The Holy Spirit comes to help Mary and the disciples. Acts 2:1-4

4. Mary is taken into heaven. Song of Songs 2:10-11

5. Mary becomes Queen of heaven. Revelation 12:1

Rise and Shine!

Jesus shows us the power of the Holy Spirit. He shared that power with Mary and his disciples. He shares it with us, too. The Holy Spirit brightens our lives in amazing ways!

What happens at the end of every night? Finish this picture. Color it with glorious colors. Then follow the code.

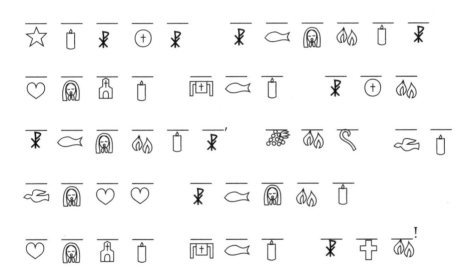

CODE

 = A   = H   = K   = O   = U

= D   = I   = L   = S   = W

= E   = J   = N   = T

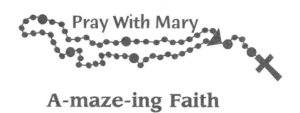

A-maze-ing Faith

The rosary connects our hearts to God. That is a wonderful thing! Sometimes, when you pray the rosary, you will feel very, very relaxed. You might not want to finish. That is okay. Just enjoy feeling relaxed.

In fact, that relaxed feeling is more than okay! It means you are resting in God. This is where peace begins—with you! Your heart fills with God's love. Then it overflows in amazing ways!

God's love is overflowing! Start at the center of this heart. Find three pathways to the outside.

Active Faith

The rosary connects our actions to love. That is another wonderful thing! The rosary helps us remember how much God loves us. That is the Good News that Jesus comes to share! God loves us and lives within us.

We are called children of God. We know that God loves us. Our actions show God's love. Then others know that God loves them, too. That is how we help Jesus with his mission!

How do we share God's love? Look at the pathways in the a-maze-ing heart. Write the letters that you find along each path.

Path 1 _____

Path 2 _____

Path 3 _____

Read these examples of the three paths. Write the correct path number in front of each example. The first is done for you.

A. **2** I share my toys.

B. ___ "You did a great job!"

C. ___ Grandmother forgets things but tells great stories.

D. ___ I play fair.

E. ___ "Please."

F. ___ We lost the game, but I won't blame any one person.

G. ___ I help vacuum the rugs.

H. ___ "Thank you."

I. ___ I pick up litter on the playground.

J. ___ I can learn about customs different than mine.

Think of your own examples. Add them to your actions today!

Confident Connections

Mary helps with Jesus' mission. She says "Yes!" to God. She shares God's love when she prays with us. When we pray with Mary, we say "Yes!" to God, too.

Mary is confident that God loves us and lives in us. Confident means sure. Are you confident God lives in us? Look at these pictures. Say them out loud. Listen carefully. Then write each word on the line below.

M +

 - d

 - t + f +

_____   _____   _____

 - mb

L + + d

&  m +

_____   _____   _____

s  + it

re +  - t - ck

N

_____   _____   _____

𝕲od

 m +

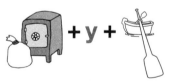 + y +

_____   _____   _____

Luke 1:46

This is the first line in a beautiful prayer of Mary's called the "Magnificat." You can read the whole prayer in Luke 1:46-55.

Creative Connections

There are many ways to help Jesus with his mission. If you can imagine a way, you can pray about it. If you can pray about it, you can help to make it happen!

Imagine this! Fill in the letters below. Hint: The pictures show you the shape of the letter and the answer itself.

1. Imagine a rosary made of b a l l __ __ n s
   that lift your prayers to God.

2. Imagine a rosary made of __ __ __ __ __
   for sharing after Mass on Sunday mornings.

3. Imagine a rosary made of __ __ __ __ __
   for sharing with people who are poor.

4. Imagine a rosary made of __ __ __ __ __ __
   for thanking the teachers at your school.

5. Imagine a rosary made of __ __ __ __ __ __ __
   for writing letters to people who are lonely.

6. Imagine a rosary made of __ __ __ __ __ __ __
   for enjoying creation!

7. Imagine a rosary made of __ __ __ __ __
   to read with your friends.

8. Imagine a rosary made of __ __ __ __ __ prints
   from your classmates, family, or friends.

Word List			
apples	books	donuts	pencils
balloons	coins	flowers	thumb

What are some more ways to help with Jesus' mission?

YOUR Connections

Make a paper-chain rosary for YOUR prayers.

You will need:

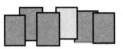 construction paper
(1 sheet of one color; 5 of another)

 scissors and ruler (or) paper cutter
(ask an adult to help)

 pencil or pen; stapler and staples

 cardboard; string or yarn

1. Turn the construction paper so the long side is at the top. *Measure strips that are 1 inch wide by 8 1/2 inches long. You should get 11 strips from each piece of construction paper.*

a. Use one color paper for the Lord's Prayer. **Cut 6 strips.**

b. Use the other color paper for the Hail Mary. **Cut 53 strips.**

c. Divide the Hail Mary strips into **six piles**.
  • One pile is for the tail. Put **3 strips** in it.
  • Five piles are for the decades on the loop. Put **10 strips** in each decade-pile.

d. Choose **five** prayer-themes. A prayer-theme is anything for which you want to pray—family, the ill, your problems—it is up to you.

e. Write a prayer-theme on each strip in a decade. Complete all five decades.

2. Form the chains.

a. To make the **tail**, start  with a Lord's Prayer strip. Form a circle and staple it. Insert a Hail Mary strip through the Lord's Prayer circle. Form a circle with the Hail Mary strip, and staple its ends. Add two more Hail Mary circles. End the tail chain with a second Lord's Prayer circle.

b. To make the big loop, make chains of 10 circles each from the five decade-piles. Connect one decade to the next with a Lord's Prayer circle.

c. By now, you should have used all the strips. You have one long chain plus the tail. You are almost finished!

3. Cut the cardboard shapes.

a. Trace the cross and triangle shapes onto a piece of paper. (Do not cut them out of this page.)

b. Cut the shapes out of the paper.

c. Place the shapes onto the cardboard. Draw around them.

d. Cut the shapes out of the cardboard and punch the holes as shown.

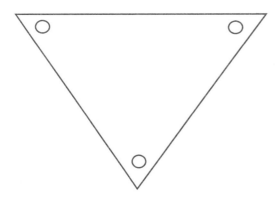

4. Use the string to finish the rosary.

a. Tie the tail to the cross and the triangle.

b. Tie the triangle to each end of the loop.

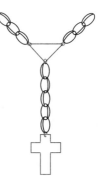

Pray With Mary

Crossword Connections

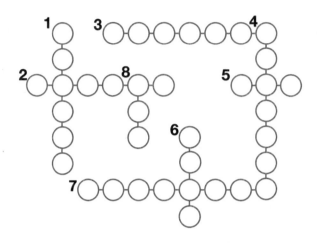

1. The _____ is named after Mary, the "Mystical Rose."

2. Long ago, monks used 150 pebbles to count 150 _____.

3. The pebbles were replaced by knots on a string, later by beads. The psalms were replaced by _____ to Mary.

4. Scripture _____ were added. They are called mysteries.

5. Joyful Mysteries show Mary's happiness and _____. Luminous Mysteries show Jesus' mission.

6. Sorrowful Mysteries show Jesus' _____.

7. _____ Mysteries show the Holy Spirit's power.

8. We honor Mary during the month of _____.

Word List	
Glorious	prayers
joy	psalms
May	rosary
pain	stories

We celebrate the rosary during the month of October.

Closing Connections

Wow! This is a lot to learn in one little book! The rosary is full of connections. Which ones do you remember? Draw a line to connect the choices below.

The rosary connects...

...our fingers...   ...to God.

... our minds...   ...to love.

... our hearts...   ...to the beads.

...our actions...   ...to prayers and Scripture.

These are BIG connections. As you grow in faith, they will get even BIGGER. Trust that! In the meantime...

Keep Connected!

Keep it handy. Keep your rosary where you will see it often. Hang it on your bedroom doorknob. Drape it over your mirror. Carry it in your pocket, backpack, or purse.

Keep in touch. Read this book again and again.

Keep it simple. Start with one decade. Choose a mystery. Or think about something that is important to you. Add more decades when you are ready.

Keep praying. Pray the Rosary anytime—morning, afternoon, evening. Pray anywhere—at home, in the car, at the park. Pray by yourself. Pray with family and friends. *Pray with Mary!*

Activity Answers

Page 4
mother

Page 5
Let there be peace on earth and let it begin with me. Amen!

Page 7
(a) 5 (b) 10 (c) 50 (d) 3 (e) 6 (f) 59

Page 9
A tangle like this is "knot" a good connection!

Page 11
1. Father; 2. Son; 3. Holy Spirit;
4. Amen

Page 14
1. The angel Gabriel; 2. Hail Mary;
3. "Lord, teach us to pray." 4. Lord's Prayer

Page 15
mysteries

Page 17
Jesus' light; my light

Page 21
1. lonely; 2. hurt; 3. angry; 4. sad;
5. afraid

Page 23
Jesus shines like the sun shines, and we will shine like the Son!

Page 24

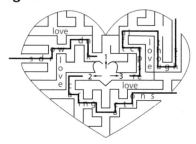

Page 25
1. kind words; 2. caring actions;
3. respectful thoughts
A. 2; B. 1; C. 3; D. 2; E. 1; F. 3; G. 2;
H. 1; I. 2; J. 3

Page 26
M + eye = **My**; Sold – d = **soul**;
magnet – t + f + eyes = **magnifies**;
thumb – mb = **the**; L + oar + d = **Lord**;
& = **and**; m + eye = **my**;
s + pear + it = **spirit**;
re + joysticks – t – ck = **rejoices**
N = **in**; **God**; m + eye = **my**;
safe + y + oar = **savior**

Page 27
1. balloons; 2. donuts; 3. coins;
4. apples; 5. pencils; 6. flowers;
7. books; 8. thumbprints

Page 30
1. rosary; 2. psalms; 3. prayers;
4. stories; 5. joy; 6. pain; 7. Glorious;
8. May

Page 31
The rosary connects our fingers to the beads, our minds to prayers and Scriptures, our hearts to God, our actions to love.